Shafts of Light

Selected Teachings of Swami Ashokananda for Spiritual Practice

Cate Cummings

Publicity & Promotion Group
7601 East 93rd Street
Kansas City, MO 64138-4206
(816) 767-0396 • Fax (816) 767-0289
Email: Cor@BookPublicity.com
Website: www.BookPublicity.com

Shafts of Light

Selected Teachings of
Swami Ashokananda
for Spiritual Practice

Compiled and Edited by
Sister Gargi and Shelley Brown

Kalpa Tree Press
New York

Kalpa Tree Press
65 East 96th Street, Suite 12D
New York, NY 10128
www.kalpatree.com

*The photograph of Swami Ashokananda on the frontispiece and back cover
are courtesy of the Vedanta Society of Northern California.*

The Rose, *1958–1966, by Jay DeFeo (1929–1989)*
Oil with wood and mica on canvas
Overall: 128 ⅞ x 92 ¼ in., 5070.6 lb.
(327.3 x 234.3 x 27.9 cm, 2300 kg)
Framed: 131 1/16 x 94 ⅜ x 5 in. (332.9 x 239.7 x 12.7 cm)
Whitney Museum of American Art, New York;
*Gift of the Estate of Jay DeFeo and purchase, with funds from the Contemporary Painting and
Sculpture Committee and the Judith Rothschild Foundation 95.170*
Photograph © Ben Blackwell, CA

Publisher's Cataloging-in-Publication Data

Shafts of light : selected teachings of Swami Ashokananda
for spiritual practice / compiled and edited by Sister
Gargi and Shelley Brown. —1st ed.
p. cm.
Includes bibliographical references.
LCCN 2003116961
ISBN 0-9706368-3-0

1. Vedanta 2. Yoga. 3. Ashokananda, Swami—
Teachings. I. Burke, Marie Louise, 1912-. II. Brown, Shelley.
B132.V3S415 2004   181'.48
QB104-200116

Book design by Fearn Cutler de Vicq

10 9 8 7 6 5 4 3 2 1
FIRST EDITION

Contents

PART TWO

SPIRITUAL PRACTICE

Finding the Spirit—Inside and Out

PART THREE

THE EXPERIENCE OF GOD

I Am the Self—Pure Consciousness—All Light

Preface

Over a period of many years, Swami Ashoka-nanda delivered hundreds of lectures on Vedanta and held half as many classes on the Upanishads, the ancient Hindu scriptures that are the seminal utterances of Vedanta philosophy itself. From the 1930s, when Swami Ashokananda arrived in the United States, until the end of 1967, when he gave his last lecture, a number of his disciples took notes during his talks. They captured verbatim his most striking, often jolting, sentences—passages that ignited for them one Vedantic teaching after another, and that would continue to spur their spiritual life.

Knowing of this habit of my fellow disciples and friends, I asked a few of them if they would make their personal notes available to me, perhaps for future publication and, at least, for certain preservation. Blessed friends! They knew the timeless value of what they held and, being free of possessiveness, they readily handed over to me their choicest selections. Shamelessly, I have hoarded that treasure like a crafty old miser ever since. But my intentions were good.

In the journal I kept during the 1960s, I find an entry in which I told Swami Ashokananda about the existence of these notes, and in which I said to him that if they were published they would make a wonderful book, helpful to devotees of all traditions and levels of spiritual maturity. I thought he would firmly say no; but instead he smiled and said, "Go ahead." That permission to put together the present book and bring it to the light of day was given almost forty years ago. I am sorry to have taken so long to share these passages from the notes of the Swami's disciples. I was perhaps waiting for them to be put into harmonious and coherent order by the expert and generous hand of my friend and editor, Dr. Shelley Brown, my colleague on this book; I think the result is well worth the wait.

Swami Ashokananda's spiritual counsel and instructions come through these passages with his characteristic force and clarity. They are for the most part verbatim, or have undergone minor editing with full attention to the meaning and cadences of the Swami's words. May this selection shed light on the reader's spiritual path.

Gargi

San Francisco, January 1, 2004

Introduction

This is a book about inner light—enlightenment—the light that floods the center of one's being in deepest meditation to bring peace and joy; the moment when all the knots of the heart unravel and one knows, truly, who one is. Vedantins call this illumined state Self-realization or God-consciousness, the experience of which brings fulfillment and overwhelming love.

Centered in this holy incandescent light, an authentic spiritual teacher can guide seekers as they stumble along the murky path of self-discovery and, with a penetrating understanding of individual needs, can help kindle the sacred fire in each heart. Swami Ashokananda was such a teacher. "His personality was like a flame," said Sister Gargi, "that could change the darkest chasms of one's mind into fields of light." In the preface to her biography of Swami Ashokananda, *A Heart Poured Out,* she wrote,

> We are all thrashing about in a dark and hurtful world, and all the while we can light

our own inextinguishable lamp of strength and wisdom by which we can see our way. This was Swami Ashokananda's faith, indeed, his knowledge, and so sure was that knowledge that he gave his life to showing us how to light our own lamps.

Words that Swami Ashokananda spoke in his lectures and classes—soul-stirring, numinous insights from the wellspring of his own experience—were noted down by his close disciples for their own spiritual practice. Selected passages from these notes are offered herein to other practitioners for the first time. Though delivered in his charming vernacular, Swami Ashokananda's spiritual instructions embody the teachings of Vedanta at their most sublime.

SWAMI ASHOKANANDA (1893–1969) was a dynamic speaker, one of the best, and he attracted a steady stream of congregants to the Vedanta Society of Northern California, which he headed from 1932 until his death in 1969. A pioneer on the Vedanta frontier, Swami Ashokananda established new Vedanta centers in Berkeley and Sacramento, developed the 2,000-acre Vedanta Retreat at Olema (still the largest in the Western Hemisphere), and built the large New Temple in San Francisco to accommodate the Society's growing membership and activities. His contributions to the Vedanta movement in America are well known, as are his lectures in print, which have become a popular source of inspiration since the first collection was published in 1970.

Less well known until recently were the struggles Swami Ashokananda endured and the obstacles he overcame to accomplish his goals, as well as his brilliance as a teacher of Vedanta to a group of dedicated and independent-minded Americans. His life and work are the subject of Sister Gargi's biography, *A Heart Poured Out*—from his days as a God-absorbed boy in village India to his decades as a God-centered monk of the Ramakrishna Order in the United States. A more intimate portrait emerges through the Swami's conversations in Sister Gargi's memoir, *A Disciple's Journal*—his words sweet and witty, probing and insightful, as he chipped away at the author's uncertainty and self-doubt. These two books by Sister Gargi reveal the strengthening impact of Swami Ashokananda's enlightened personality on her own and his other disciples' lives.

Shafts of Light includes more than eight hundred spiritual directives that Swami Ashokananda imparted to his disciples over three decades of training.

"Shafts" accurately describes teachings that so cleanly hit their mark: ego-stabbing thrusts and penetrating insights to prod listeners (and readers) to rise above the selfish limitations and small-mindedness that hinder spiritual growth, in concert with sharply focused counsel to guide and encourage the spiritual ascent.

The theme of transcendence in these passages will appeal to readers who want the essence of spiritual life without the trappings of popular religion. Swami Ashokananda taught a pure Vedanta that had little to do with Hindu customs, which he felt were out of place at American centers. He never permitted his disciples to kowtow, and he applauded traditional Western values. "I want first-rate Americans," he would thunder, "not fifth-rate Hindus!" His insistence on cultural authenticity for Americans was an example of his genius as a teacher of Vedanta in the West.

Shafts of Light is intended for readers in all stages of spiritual maturity. In ascending order, the book is divided into "Spiritual Perspectives," "Spiritual Practice," and "The Experience of God." Within short chapters, which highlight the main themes, passages have been grouped to present a particular teaching from different angles—a prismatic effect that may shed more light on the reader's understanding. Whether contemplated in an organized fashion or browsed, *Shafts of Light* offers spiritual sustenance in every passage and, in abundance, on every page.

NOT ALL READERS are familiar with Vedanta philosophy. A few key concepts are introduced in the brief discussion of Swami Ashokananda's teachings below in three parts. Illustrative quotations are all in the Swami's words from *Shafts of Light.*

Am I This Body, Mind, and Ego?

As a spiritual teacher, Swami Ashokananda was a compassionate guide. An adherent of Advaita (nondual) Vedanta, he was aware of the divinity of all life and he saw in his disciples their potential perfection. Beyond their human quirks and ego-bound foibles he beheld the pure Spirit, and his role as a teacher was to polish the mirror of each disciple's perception to reflect this inner light.

It is as a student seeking enlightenment that the reader should approach the Swami's instructions in Part One to transcend the body, mind, and ego. Only when the gross elements are refined do they become instruments of spiritual perception. "When you have made every effort to transcend the lower state," Swami Ashokananda taught his disciples, "that is the beginning of the higher mind. You become quiet within, the recipient of grace." Freeing the mind from the beck and call of the senses is a battle for self-mastery that is unceasing but must be tackled early on. The ego, or selfish I-consciousness, will try to prevail, but it, too, must be transformed: "When you are spiritually awakened, every simple action is felt to be not of the ego but of the Spirit."

A life in the Spirit is a different kind of life. Daily activities that are usually motivated by the drive for ego gratification and validation must be reoriented to purify the mind. Gradually one learns how to tune all feelings, thoughts, and actions to the spiritual goal, and how to remain calm. "Everything you do is a ritual. If your heart is in it, it becomes spiritual," the Swami assured his students. With practice, the mind becomes serene—the vehicle of spiritual intelligence. "You will find that in back of all this agitation of the senses there is a calm mind, and through this calm mind all is known."

As the Spirit gains ascendancy, the external loses its sway. "A true sign of spiritual growth is a state in which we are not so affected by conditions of the body and mind." Conflicts, suffering, illness, even the experience of death, cease to be overwhelming when they lead to a deeper reality. "Welcome life; welcome death," Swami Ashokananda said. "Don't dance to a little tune." Vedanta has the perspective of eternity, beyond human limitations, in which nothing short of finding the Spirit will do.

Finding the Spirit—Inside and Out

"In spiritual life the way is to change ourselves, to change our own reaction to things. It is our reaction that makes all the trouble." Swami Ashokananda's instructions in Part Two are an invitation to change whatever in oneself is petty, weak, selfish, conceited, and faultfinding, into a personality that is strong, affirmative, purposeful, courageous, and loving. "Burn out the clutter in your consciousness," he advised. "Don't be afraid of the struggle."

The first chapter is a simple exhortation to begin. Spiritualizing oneself is not an easy task. Success comes only with sustained eagerness. "Our whole problem is laziness," Swami Ashokananda said. "After five minutes of prayerful effort we expect God to come fluttering down." But the purpose of spiritual struggle is to achieve full consciousness—the illumined state. "Hang on," Swami

Ashokananda encouraged his disciples in their moments of weakness; no effort is wasted. "Even though you see no result, you are awakening the higher mind." Don't be downhearted—your practice should be joyous, for struggle itself is a sign of God's grace. Through struggle the mind becomes quiet, and when the mind is perfectly still, "the soul becomes Spirit."

Vedanta is a search for truth but "our perception, our understanding, is only skin deep." The ordinary mind has its limitations. It sees only the face where the illumined mind sees "God, peeping through the eyes." "To the extent that we learn to feel for others—to that extent we transcend our limitations," the Swami said. The old habits of mind must be broken to see the Spirit behind the face—the luminous Being within.

"According to Vedanta, every person, every being, is perfect." Far from being critical, the spiritual aspirant should have no animosity, should treat every person, every being, as God Himself. "No righteous indignation—don't backbite," Swami Ashokananda warned; also be kind to all living beings, have a sense of humor, forget slights, be forgiving, don't dwell on defects. Let the Lord do the judging, and see in yourself and all others the resplendent Self.

I Am the Self—Pure Consciousness—All Light

"Profound depths are within us. There is no difference between God and our divine Self." The Swami's lessons in Part Three are aimed at Self-realization—how to discover one's true Self, or Atman, as identical with the Spirit, or Brahman. This is the goal of Advaita Vedanta. The spiritual seeker must reach very high and go very deep to achieve this goal, but the first step is to quiet the restless mind: "Be still, O mind, and know that I am the Self."

In Vedanta there are time-honored disciplines to control the mind, concentrate it, and bring it to a one-pointed meditation. To these Swami Ashokananda added fresh insights from his own spiritual experience. Groups of passages in the text clarify intuitive teachings such as these: "Meditation is not simply thinking about God. It is an actual perception of the presence of God," and "Meditation is not imagination; it is the anticipation of the Real." There are no set formulas on how to make the leap from thinking to meditation, or how to achieve God-vision ("It just happens," he said)—but Swami Ashokananda's instructions point the way.

No less compelling are Swami Ashokananda's teachings on the indwelling Spirit. On the formless

God, he instructed his disciples, "Within you, in the center of your being, is a flame—a light without any smoke. That is Brahman. Meditate on Him." On the supreme goal of Advaita Vedanta, he told them, "Meditate on your God, but also on your Self. That is what you really are." Words such as the following, perhaps from his own experience, must have inspired in his disciples a vivid expectation: "Miraculous things begin to happen when you think of the true nature of the Self. You will be surprised to find how the Self has become an illumined force within you."

In Vedanta philosophy, the concept of ignorance replaces that of sin, and ignorance is maya—the cosmic veil that obscures one's vision of spiritual reality. Swami Ashokananda urged his disciples to liberate themselves from this earthbound oblivion: "You have denied your own true nature. Set fire to the rope that is binding you. Make the transformation!" Beyond the limitations of I-consciousness is pure identity—"when God is both within and without, even God is gone. What is left is beyond words."

The simplicity of enlightenment is glimpsed in the final passage of *Shafts of Light:* "The great ones do not do anything but this: they recognize the divinity in you and that divinity responds and comes out. Light responds to light." This is Swami Ashokananda speaking, not about himself, for he was too modest for that, but about the great saints he had once known. It was left for Sister Gargi to describe, in *A Heart Poured Out,* the light she saw in her teacher's eyes.

WHEN SISTER GARGI asked me to collaborate on this book, she showed me a large suitcase filled with notebooks, her own and those of other disciples of Swami Ashokananda. On top were typewritten pages in a binder labeled "first rough draft," containing excerpts that Sister Gargi had chosen and edited in an earlier time. As we worked on this text and added more passages from the notebooks, I found these lively teachings coming to mind and illuminating my thoughts throughout the day. This confirmed in my experience what Sister Gargi had said all along— here was a spiritual treasure trove.

The accuracy of the text in *Shafts of Light* owes much to Sister Gargi's unerring eye for precision in language, her ear for Swami Ashokananda's cadence, and her knowledge of his teachings. We finished compiling and editing the manuscript, with Sister Gargi's approval on a draft of this introduction, before her death on January 20, 2004. The elegant preface was her last piece of writing.

A passage in *Shafts of Light* seems to fit Sister Gargi's life in the Spirit, its natural grace: "There are those upon whose face God has written in His own hand 'Mine.' They are not of this world; they are His." It was always a privilege, as well as a delight, to be in the company of this rare soul. To this I add my joy in working with Sister Gargi on her final three books, and in her friendship—indelible memories that summon my deep and abiding gratitude.

Shelley Brown

New York, February 22, 2004

PART ONE

SPIRITUAL PERSPECTIVES

Am I This Body, Mind, and Ego?

I
The Gross Body

Am I this body, this weak mind? Why should I not invoke the powerful presence within me?

Through identification with the body, we have become as gross as the body itself.

We are like pigs in this world, all the time squealing and trying to consume sense objects.

The body is too close to us; it is squeezing our being out, as it were.

We carry the legacies of all the birds, beasts, and savages. These experiences stay and leave marks on our mind. Life is checkered with these marks—some good, some bad.

In instinct we are with animals; in reason we are with men; in higher intuition we are with the Spirit.

Friends, we should by no means live on this lower level of reality. It is full of misery.

If you have great willpower and if your mind is pure, then with a little effort you can separate yourself from this body.

If you learn not to meet all the demands of the body, there is a chance that you can rise above the body. How can you rise above the body if you continually give in to its demands?

Free yourself from being ordered about by the body. Even with a little effort you will see that you can live above its attractions; then you will know that it is literally true that you can live and move and have your being in Brahman. Transcendence is necessary.

Through discrimination, you have continually to remind yourself that you are not the body or the mind but pure Spirit. When you eat, say, "It is not I who am eating; it is the body that is eating." Some do better and say, "It is an offering to the divinity that is in me." At first the joy goes out of eating; afterward, another kind of joy comes—eating has changed.

To say "I am not the body; I am not the mind" cannot leave a deep impression as long as the sense of worldliness exists. Don't be a hypocrite in your spiritual efforts.

In order to have interior vision, the senses have to come away from external vision.

You will find that in back of all this agitation of the senses there is a calm mind, and through this calm mind all is known.

A few meager rays peep through the senses; but within, a million suns are ablaze.

The more the senses close, the more the gate of heaven opens and you see the luminous form of God.

The Spirit will give you no rest: the body and mind have to surrender themselves to the Spirit. Only then comes peace.

Remember, the Self is not connected with the body sense. It subsists in itself. It shines in its own glory.

The body comes and goes like clouds against the sky; the eternal Spirit remains. We are seeing only part of the picture.

All this emotional wealth of man is but a faint imitation of the exquisite, excruciating love of our infinite soul for the infinite God.

The joy of the Spirit is infinitely superior to anything this body and mind can bring to you.

Beautiful is the body of God, this universe, but its finer aspects are hidden from those who are blinded by the vanities of life.

The soul is all-conscious, whereas the mind and body are totally unconscious.

Every single particle of the body, mind, and universe is an individuation of Brahman.

2
The Slavish/Bullying Mind

The mind is a slave of the body. It just repeats what the body says and what the body wants.

Where do you think the mind is? In the average man it is a little in the mind, a little in the heart, but 90 percent in the muscles, in the mouth, and below the waist—on the purely physical level.

Our mind takes the character of that on which it dwells. If the mind thinks of material things all the time, it will become as gross as matter.

The mind is a miserable stenographer who keeps a record of what the senses and the body do. But when you rise above the body, the mind also rises up.

The mind is the sense of otherness.

The mind is nothing but ignorance continually vibrating.

We get ideas and these ideas get frozen into attitudes.

The mind is so hard that an atomic bomb will not make a dent in it, but meditation will.

⁂

Despair and discouragement are two of the luxuries in which the mind indulges.

One becomes identified with the states of the mind. We dance to the tune of the mind.

When the mind takes an unhappy turn you say, "I am unhappy." You are not unhappy; the mind is unhappy.

Against the calm, luminous soul, the mind dances its dance—and we identify with the mind.

When the mind becomes calm, you see deep into everything.

⁂

The finite and the Infinite will never shake hands.

The object is to free the mind from the body.

Ride the body and mind; do not let the body and mind ride you.

If you are not the body or the mind, nothing can set a limit to you. The sense of limitation comes only from the body and the mind.

The mind is not a sovereign thing; it is the instrument of the soul.

The natural tendency of the mind is toward God, not toward evil. If we take off what is imposed on the mind, it will fly to Truth.

※

It is better to evoke the higher mind than to wrestle with the lower mind. How? By dwelling on that which makes the mind higher. Infinite love and dignity are there.

I will make a wild speculation: modern people do not delve into the unconscious in order to understand the mind; they do so because the conscious state has become unbearable.

It is a highly dangerous game to try to probe into your own mind. You must not do it.

"Don't dig too deeply in the ground lest a cobra come out."—Bengali saying.

Until you have great control of your mind, don't study it. Dwell on God.

With the conscious mind alone we can reach the highest, without the use of the unconscious mind.

If you want to commune with God, it is done with the enlargement and expansion of your conscious mind. This very mind becomes superconscious.

3

The Agony of Thinking

Very few are willing to undertake the agony of thinking. We are not superstitious people; we are intelligent—but thoughtful? No!

Those who say "It is the will of God" just say so to stop any further thinking.

Until you become confused, you do not try to think.

However intelligent we are, our whole thinking is awfully stupid.

Common sense is often no sense at all.

When we are ignorant about something, the idea we have about that thing is usually the opposite of what it really is.

Ignorance always functions by denying the thing of which we are ignorant.

Don't make an argument of your ignorance.

Stubbornness is weakness because the stubborn person feels that if he gives in, he is gone. A strong man is flexible.

Stubbornness is not courage; it is a kink in the brain.

4
The Interference of Ego

In the same way that a few fingers can shut off the sun, the ego can hide the Self.

If I forget myself, resplendent things come. The ego hides them like a small, dark cloud.

If we can forget our own tremendous interest in the ego, extraordinary powers of the Spirit will manifest.

If our ego does not interfere, our heart and intellect act under divine guidance.

If this little "ego-I" did not interfere, we would perceive God Himself. The Self, by Itself, is complete and perfect.

Whichever way we go, the contrariness of our own nature stands in our way.

Egotism can ruin everything. You have to learn that egotism has no place in spiritual life, in the form of either insolence or despair.

Try to get rid of the ego. A close watch should be kept all along the path. The ego may take the form of superiority or inferiority. Try to humiliate it and get rid of it. The ego is an imposter masquerading as ourselves. We are the Self, an entirely different thing.

It is unfortunate not to meet with humiliation, because humiliation is the best way to get rid of this "I."

The ego cannot thrive unless it is given food to feed on. Remember this: don't ever let any food be given to it, either by yourself or by others.

Beware of any outgoing tendency of the mind, of so-called doing good with the egotistic sense of helping anyone. God alone helps man.

Any idea of yourself except the true idea of Self is egotism. A man who whines is an egotist and a man who shouts is also an egotist; neither of these attitudes is acceptable to God. But there is another approach, a childlike approach; that is the kind of thing God wants.

Ego and desire—the two are almost interchangeable. We should whack at both of them.

※

The ego is like a rainbow. The light of the Self is thrown on the mists that arise from the turmoil of the body and the mind.

The ego is just a reflector and it is hard for us to distinguish the reflector from what is reflected.

To think the ego does anything is an illusion. All the ego does is to put its stamp on what really is coming from the Lord.

※

We have forgotten our infinitude. A time comes when we are rescued from our small unit of individuality—our little intelligence, our ego, our small space in time. What remains? Perfection.

First be established in union with the divine Self; then forget the little self, the ego, entirely.

When you are spiritually awakened, every simple action is felt to be not of the ego but of the Spirit.

Humility is the essential thing in one's spiritual progress.

Humility is unself-consciousness.

True humility and self-abnegation come only when there arises that perpetual, loving consciousness of divinity pervading all—then the ego shrivels.

In some sane moment, we suddenly shift our ground and find we are not this "I."

5
The Human Handicap

There is a hunger, an unseemly hunger, in the senses.

The senses perceive correctly only when there is no greed behind them.

Ajnana, ignorance, is the texture of our present existence.

Give up the terrible mistake of thinking of everything in terms of this existence. You have to get rid of this idea; it is a disease. Until you have learned to perceive yourself as free from the body, you do not know how even to speak of philosophy and religion.

We are so contrary. We howl "There is no God!" until we are exhausted and cannot perceive Him.

As long as we suffer from this terrible tendency of not seeing God, we will see only this world of forms.

The world of forms is around our neck and we have no peace.

Know for certain that whenever you are interested in anything relative—with form—it is selfish from beginning to end.

Most friends are just companions in pleasure seeking.

By taking on certain relationships to others, you also impose limitations upon yourself. By saying "This is my wife," you are also saying that you are a man.

Our love of human beings is nothing but a distortion of the love of God. The same attraction and emotions, directed to God, become divine.

God has a human side as long as our own humanity is not free from impurity.

For years and years we approach God in human terms. Most of us approach Him for earthly benefits. But if we are sincere and approach Him for spiritual things, He responds.

God is neither feminine nor masculine. The music of the universe, rhythmic and dynamic, is represented as God as Mother—*Shakti,* the Primal Energy.

Get rid of your own form, the body. Freed of all forms, everything is God.

If we can somehow make all forms appear as two-dimensional, flat coverings disguising the Infinite One, then we will see the divinity behind all beings and all things, exquisite and adorable.

Nature, when we come close, is only a film of paint. Our human nature is like a painted film. Wake up! You have been dreaming an evil dream.

Is there any method or process of waking up from this dream? No, you just wake up.

6
The Imperfection of Time

Whatever is in time is imperfect; it cannot be true. If you mix up the search for truth with worldly living, you get into a snarl.

To be carried along by this powerful current of time is not true existence.

We are designed to leave one moment of existence behind so that we can have the next moment of experience. That is time.

If you try to find yourself, all you find is a passing condition.

Have a sense of time unpunctured by the passing phenomena of the day.

We have become creatures of time because we have forgotten eternity. Time is the opposite of eternity.

When a man does not do things in terms of eternity, he is drifting; there is nothing to anchor him.

Unless time is hooked into eternity, we feel adrift; we have no solace in our hearts.

The easiest way to destroy time is to fall in love with He who is Eternal.

Living in time, you will now and then begin to taste eternity.

A person who is not afflicted by time—he alone has patience, endurance.

Do you know that patience is another name for eternity? Impatience is a state of mind that is to be condemned in every phase of life.

Do you know what is behind impatience? We are not willing to undertake as much trouble as we should. We want to get it over with quickly and get on to something else. Impatience can do you a great deal of harm.

Our history tears us to pieces. Drop it as you do a dream when you wake up.

Our memories have made slaves of us.

Old friends—they smell of death.

The whole world is like *Alice in Wonderland*, a madhouse. As long as you see everything slide by in reasonable sequence, one thing firmly tied to another, you are a bound person. When you realize there is no sequence, no congruity, you are free.

7

The Agony of Conflict

Conflict bothers people today, but without conflict no growth is attained. "Complacent as a cow"— is there any growth in that? I do not say that every conflict is desirable, but conflict in itself is not always bad.

Have conflict—what of it? Conflict will be what will save you.

If you have a conflict or misunderstanding among yourselves, never try to solve it by deciding who is right or wrong. That would do in a court of law, but justice has no place in spiritual life. Transcend it— just forget. It is not that the other person admits he is wrong, but that you are friendly to him; that is your triumph. But won't the other person continue to do wrong? No. The very fact that you forgot will change him. The teacher, whose job it is to improve people, can talk to him and show him his fault.

The most important ingredient of wisdom is a sense of proportion.

Problems are not solved; problems are transcended. If you think you have solved them, then you are making peace with your present condition, which is a compromise.

Most of our problems are phases, qualities of our own self-existence. When we change our state of existence, all the problems pertaining to our previous state will be left behind. Once you have grasped this principle, you can leave behind problem after problem.

Purity in the highest sense comes when we are not aware of any kind of conflicting element within ourselves; when our being flourishes and functions without impediment, and on the highest level.

8

The Secrets of Spiritual Growth

Life is short, but the art of spiritual unfoldment is long and very difficult to practice. What of it? Do you realize what you are undertaking? The finite is going to the Infinite. What more do you want?

Spiritual growth is very, very slow. What is needed is continuity of effort.

Spiritual growth is infinitely slow, even when an aspirant struggles sincerely. Great patience is necessary. As you meditate, live the life.

Don't make your spiritual growth difficult. Forget all the clutter around you. Hit on the essentials. Remain steady.

Steadiness, endurance—that power is the basis of spiritual growth.

Faith, patience, and endurance! If you have these three and if you struggle, you will be safe—not comfortable, but safe and secure. Without these, you will be ruined.

When you have exhausted all the powers of your will and still do not give up, something higher wakes up. More power comes. This is the secret of spiritual achievement.

Insecurity is a very opportune time for spiritual growth. You search for something steady; you try to find resources within yourself.

Reversal of values is deadly.

A true sign of spiritual growth is a state in which we are not so affected by conditions of the body and mind, not so agitated by temptations or temporary disturbances.

The most potent asset in spiritual life is the constant thought of oneself as entirely separate from the body and mind. And this must not remain an intellectual concept but must develop into an unshakable conviction and then into a vivid experience. Until this separation has taken place, spiritual growth is practically impossible.

Concern about the past is one of the greatest obstructions to spiritual growth ("Oh, if only I had not done that"). Make a bundle of the past and drop it.

Without character there cannot be morality; without morality there cannot be any spiritual growth.

I am more and more convinced that character is the greater part of spirituality. Character is that by which a thing appears to us as it is.

Tapas, austerity, comes from the root word "to heat." Our normal or accustomed nature is in conflict with our higher nature. When we struggle, we create friction between the ideal and the normal state, which does not want to let us go. The effort of this struggle is necessary, like rubbing two sticks together to generate heat. Out of this heat a new power comes, a new light comes, and much impurity is consumed.

Spiritual development is always characterized by peace; that which is crooked becomes straight.

Spiritual growth is accession to greater and greater joy. Awake or asleep, the mind is continually yearning for God.

He will know God who can say, "I have plunged myself into God. Even though I have not seen Him, still I trust Him."

Practice with obedience and trust, and you will make headway.

The wonderful thing about spiritual gain is that no power on earth can take it from you.

Everyone is following a pattern; and when that pattern is fully expressed, one reaches perfection.

Spiritual growth consists in withdrawing from the manifold and proceeding toward the One.

As you make spiritual progress, you begin to lose consciousness of the outside. You feel greater and greater unity, calmness, purity, and freedom—as if you had stepped out of this sphere. Time becomes tinctured with eternity.

You cannot achieve the sense of unity with God if you have the slightest sense of your own individuality.

We have become involved in the derivatives. We have not gone to the source of things.

Trace your way back. Go to unity. Spiritual progress means to regain your true divine nature.

The divine Self, the Atman, is forever separate from matter, from the body. It can never be connected. It is a distinct entity. We have but to look back, remembering, to find the ever glorious, exquisite One.

Never calculate your spiritual growth; it is an obstruction to do so.

Progress in spiritual life is simply a matter of more and more control of the mind—of higher and higher states of mind.

9
The Higher Mind

The higher mind reflects Spirit, eternal verities. The lower mind reflects matter, objects of desire.

The lower mind does not perceive Spirit. There is another mind that has to wake up. It is through your struggle, your suffering, and your effort to rise beyond matter that you awaken your higher mind.

When the worldly mind has become thin, the higher mind shines through. This higher mind never tells anything but the truth; it cannot make a mistake. Higher reason is the same as mystical consciousness.

The mind has got layers and layers. It is larger and larger toward its base. The individual mind in its totality is in no way to be distinguished from the divine mind.

Whatever succeeds in awakening the higher mind—

bring it out. Keep the mind away from its accustomed grooves.

The more you dwell on the truth of God, the more your mind will come alive.

When your spiritual intelligence is awakened, you will find that all this so-called intelligence of man is purely mechanical.

When you have made every effort to transcend the lower state, that is the beginning of the higher mind. You become quiet within, the recipient of grace.

God's grace is rare because of the state of the mind. Wet objects do not catch fire.

When the mind is perfectly still, the soul becomes Spirit.

You will experience the higher mind in moments of great calmness and serenity when you feel no restlessness and no desire. A little experience of that sort will convince you and will leave a deep impression.

10
The Light of Consciousness

The body and mind are lower modes of consciousness. But when one is identified with the Infinite—the living light of consciousness—the body and mind vanish along with all other forms.

Consciousness does not belong to the mind as you know it.

It is the consciousness behind the physical counterpart with which you can see, hear, and touch God; that consciousness is pure, a part of the original consciousness.

Consciousness is like light: it watches everything as a spectator and never becomes contaminated.

Consciousness is the essence of spiritual substance. Consciousness is not seen easily. Life, yes, but life and consciousness as we perceive them are not identical. The change comes within us and there is a simultaneous change in our perception of reality.

All perception takes place in consciousness. When you have the perception of God, the external goes away.

The light of consciousness is God, the Spirit.

When there is any consciousness other than that of God, it is not religion. There can be no compromise. Let us admit the ideal to be realized whether or not we have gained any ground at all.

Consciousness has to be transformed by constant reiteration of the truth.

If there is a strong desire to go toward the light, you must literally develop wings. To dwell in the realm of pure consciousness, you must submerge all impulses of hatred, anger, jealousy, and desire to hurt others; under all circumstances, you must remain calm and controlled. As you bring in more light, evil tendencies will go.

As our spiritual consciousness grows, the sense of luminosity grows more and more and shadows disappear. That light is His being, interpenetrating everything.

God is the holiest of the holy, absolutely pure. He can be reflected only in pure consciousness, and pure consciousness cannot exist without the purest bodily and mental life.

Why does my thought reflect the universe? Why are the most distant stars a part of my mind? It is because the state of my consciousness is as large as the universe. If I were as small as I appear to be, this vast universe could not be a part of my knowledge.

True knowledge comes when we investigate the knower of things and not the things to be known.

Consciousness is that which knows Itself and is known by Itself. Spirit is Consciousness. The true "I" is Being-Consciousness-Bliss—joy itself.

Being is the thing, not thinking.

11
The Resplendent Self

Your self is the miraculous Self. When you seek the things of the lower mind, you are subject to the world of law. But when you seek the things of the higher mind—divine things, spiritual things beyond matter—you enter a realm of miracles and grace.

Miraculous things will begin to happen when you think of the true nature of the Self. You will be surprised to find how the Self has become an illumined force within you.

Nature is the vesture of God. Beyond nature's mechanical laws are higher laws that are much more flexible; from there miracles come.

Suppose you have gone beyond nature and feel the movement of divine grace in your life: miracles happen, miracles of the mind. Your mind is protected from evil tendencies; that is the great miracle.

Because I know your real Self—not the flesh and
blood of you but the Infinite One who is within—I
love every hair on your head. Truly your body is a
temple of God. I see the real you.

It is the reality of the Spirit that lends its beauty, its
sweetness, its sense of oneness, to the world of phenomena.

This resplendent Self exists in all forms.

When we know the Self, we become master of all
that is.

If you say "I am the Self," you will find that the real
Self begins to affirm itself.

"All truth is within me": this is knowledge. I am the
witness, the spectator. I am that infinite effulgence
against which the universe is dancing.

Be the witness. All is play—the whole universe is
play. Watch it. Then everything brings truth.

12
The Secrets of Suffering

To suffer cheerfully is not just to suffer; it is to conquer suffering. This is much better than to be relieved of suffering. Relieved of suffering, you are the same weak being; conquer suffering and you become victorious forever.

You should be ready to suffer. If you are a coward, suffering will be painful. If you are not a coward, it might be superficially painful but it will wake up something within you.

When life is rubbed hard through struggle and suffering, a hidden beauty emerges; that life becomes fragrant and delights all.

Sweetness is sugarcoating. Until you are put under pressure, you do not call on your inner strength. Blessed are those under God's pressure who are forced to bring out their own strength.

Without suffering, you don't progress. When you understand this, pain is a blessing.

Suffering and misery are a part of existence; let them do their job. Rise above them; then comes exaltation.

Welcome pain as an opportunity. Think that it has a purpose. Nothing can happen without a purpose.

Without the darkness of pain, pleasure does not glow. Life is checkered.

The dark days in which we take no pleasure and seem to be getting nowhere are not wasted. Those are the days we accomplish the most.

Pain and pleasure should not always be identified with evil and good. Pain will make us rebel against the state of things as they are. A person deepens through pain. This is the first spiritual awakening.

Whatever comes to you, accept it with grace.

Suffering is the fate of man; you have to have your share.

People *like* to suffer. They like the bitter taste. Don't in the name of spurious sentiment shout and exclaim and get excited about it.

When the body becomes the instrument of the soul, it does not complain.

Illness destroys many bondages of life. Nothing is wasted.

Even illness borne cheerfully becomes an austerity. Austerity must be practiced or you do not attain spiritual truth.

In spiritual realization you do not leave behind anything that is worthwhile. All becomes known in its infinite fullness.

Life has a purpose whether we know it or not. If you say, "Well, I cannot accomplish any more, so what is the use of living?" the very fact that you are bearing your sufferings with fortitude is itself an achievement. You probably would be surprised to know that our greatest lessons are learned not through outward accomplishment but by bearing futility with great endurance. There you really gain the most. When outside there is nothing; when the body is weak; when even the mind is not contributing anything except for its tremendous power of stability—then you can really achieve something. When old age comes, disease comes, and difficulties arise, if you have the power of endurance to remain calm and to bear your burden without being bowed down by it, that will be your greatest achievement.

Here in this life you have to reach the point where you have stopped the power and the progress of the forces that drag you down. That point you must reach.

At the end of life you should be able to say, "Yes, the sun came, and the rain. I've been enriched by life's experience. The harvest has been abundant."

You feel sorrow and misery through the mind, but you are not the mind. The Spirit is beyond both body and mind, untouched by them.

If any loss or suffering comes to you, give it a twist. Just say, "This suffering cannot affect me: I am the Spirit."

13

What Is Death?

Live so that when death comes you can embrace it in the right spirit.

Welcome life; welcome death. Don't dance to a little tune.

Welcome everything: "I am not afraid!" He who has made his bed on the ocean is not afraid of a few drops of water. All beings dwell in the ocean of God.

If you rise above life, you also rise above death and the life after death.

Disease may come, and death, but think of them as an austerity. Offer your suffering to God. Offer your bereavement to God. All becomes sweet.

As a river that flows for thousands and thousands of

miles eventually finds peace in the bosom of the sea, so our being—restless and continuously moving on—eventually finds peace in God.

There are those upon whose face God has written in His own hand "Mine." They are not of this world; they are His.

A devotee is never lost once he has claimed God as his own.

The God of death should know that he can snatch away the body, even the mind, but he cannot touch the Spirit.

The dying person's view of death is that there is no death.

Be unidentified with both life and death. Go beyond time.

When you can *truthfully* say "I want nothing for myself," that instant you will be free; you will feel your separation from the body.

If you knew what you really are, what happens to your body and mind would not concern you at all.

We can wake ourselves up any moment. The story does not have to finish. As a matter of fact, the story never does end.

Remember, the Real undergoes no change. It will never come to an end.

What is death for a spiritual person? The soul finds that everything is spiritual, that the only thing to do is to search for God.

Death is a misunderstanding. It is conquered by the realization that we do not really die. The soul is immortal.

Hold the mind to a clear perception and you will perceive yourself as the deathless Spirit.

He who never sleeps, the eye that never closes, the bellows of the tempestuous sea—God is all this: designer, substance, sustainer, and destroyer. All this you will perceive.

Be like Shiva: still as death, indifferent to the mad dance of destruction, eternal, timeless. Witness all calmly. See the eternal Being alone—no one else, nothing else.

14
What Is Religion?

Always think of religion as the direct perception of God.

The main function of religion is to bring you to God.

Religion is the enunciation of truths pertaining to God, the Spirit.

Religion is a departure from the stupid world of unreality. It teaches the ways and means by which we can go to the very root of ignorance and cut it there.

Religion is not a matter of opinion and discussion; it is a matter of experience and practice.

Infinite and manifold are the forms of God. In whatever way one wishes to see Him, He comes.

The Lord's message comes in many ways and, for a long, long time, it does not come directly from Him.

Sects are the outer trappings of universal eternal truths.

Give up your little prejudices. Only a fool would think God is different because of different names and forms.

Old patterns must be broken and old modes of thought changed. God is to be found not only in temples, in churches, in holy men, and in seers of God—though no doubt there may be special manifestations in these places—but in *all* places everywhere, and in *all* beings and things. There was a man in a prison cell who, though bodily confined, so freed his mind by thinking of God alone that he saw Him alone. The bars vanished and even the walls, and everywhere there was light, shimmering light.

There is only one church to build: your own being. Make your being so attractive that God will want to reside in it always and make His presence felt.

Whatever works for you for the time being, that is true for you.

Everything you do is a ritual. If your heart is in it, it becomes spiritual.

All religions are the same. How you practice is the important thing.

A religion needs people of spiritual experience. Otherwise, it is just a show.

15
Who Is a Seer?

You have to find the truth about God from someone who has personal experience.

This, friends, is what you should do if you are interested in religion: find out the condition of a person who lives in God.

In this world it is difficult to find someone who knows God and will speak about Him. Should you find such a person but fail to appreciate his words, he—the knower of God—quiets down.

Fools find reality to be the world; seers find reality to be God.

A seer conveys through his speech the spark of truth. His speech is charged with power and substance. It becomes lodged in your heart.

A man of Self-Knowledge exists like the wind—a blown leaf with no direction of its own. His life is one continual benefit to others, an infinitely inspiring source of well-being. Wherever he is becomes a holy place.

The lack of eternity is death. As long as you are not eternal, you are nothing. Nothing short of being a seer of God will do.

PART TWO

SPIRITUAL PRACTICE

Finding the Spirit—Inside and Out

I
Begin

This is the time to practice, to sow the seeds—then you will reap a bumper crop.

You do not become spiritual naturally. Those who are spiritual now have done their climbing.

Whenever you undertake any practice, don't make it a clumsy habit. Elevate its dignity. Keep it alive. That is why reverence and faith are necessary.

There has to be a method in spiritual life. Everything has a method. If you want to be a singer, you must cultivate your voice, take lessons, and practice. You cannot just live a haphazard life and become a great singer. How much more careful you must be in spiritual life if you want the divine music to begin to sing!

Never have the idea that you will practice for a time and then give up. Anything of eternal value must be approached with the idea of timelessness. You must say, "It is for all time and I will do it!"

2
Make an Effort

The moment you say, "I am weak, I am nothing, only God can do it"—that moment you take leave of self-effort.

Start on the basis of your own effort. Go about knowing the truth in an intelligent way. Make use of all that will help—scriptures and teachers.

You will find at last that no one can help you. The help will come from within yourself.

One attains success only if one makes an effort. If God is not gracious to begin with, He will *become* gracious.

Our whole problem is laziness. After five minutes of prayerful effort we expect God to come fluttering down. We expect too much from the grace of God.

Our trouble is that we catch hold of the lowest rung

of the ladder and there we wait, thinking that some-one else will do the rest for us. Think again: are you not cheating yourself this way?

Our troubles in spiritual life are symptoms of our lack of enthusiasm. One sure way to overcome spir-itual difficulties is to come in contact with people who are eagerly seeking God and learn from them.

Don't be half-hearted. Have the patience of a great scholar pursuing his subject through the years, untir-ingly and with enthusiasm. We should have that kind of patience and enthusiasm for reaching God. It is our unwillingness that is the trouble.

Never slacken your effort. Do your best. Spiritual effort is your own problem, yours alone. Don't com-pare.

Never compare yourself with anybody else. Wish all well. Enjoy each day's spiritual life. That is how one realizes the highest.

We cannot live as complacently as we do and expect to achieve or attain.

Something greater than your present state has to enter into you. Only then will you be stirred up to make a spiritual effort.

There are no definite methods that lead to the realization of the Self. It just happens. But those who attain it have a great *eagerness.*

Conviction is what most people call faith. Real conviction, when it comes, will not let you alone—you become a lunatic in your pursuit of God.

3

Hang On

Burn out the clutter in your consciousness. Don't be afraid of struggle.

In spiritual life even a loss is a gain if you hold on to your spiritual practices and don't give up.

You must not lose courage. You must not lose hope. Above all, you must be very, very patient.

Determination without patience is destructive.

If we fail and are unhappy, it is due to our own faint-heartedness.

A strong person does not give up fighting. If you hold on, you will find that all the things that are against you now will become favorable.

The external always yields to a person who has done his internal battle victoriously.

If you cultivate your inner nature, fear will go. Whatever you cultivate, you can achieve.

Success in the material world is uncertain, but an adequate effort in spiritual life is always certain of success.

To go from success to success makes a person weak—if failure comes, he will suddenly collapse. A true soldier is he who has fought many battles, has been defeated many times.

It does not matter to what depth of degradation you have fallen. Even there say, "I am the infinite Spirit." Every time you fall, get up.

Be brave. Never mind failure. Go on—make a new mold. Failure succeeded by another effort brings more courage and perseverance. Failure becomes a stepping-stone.

In climbing mountains, going down is also going for-ward. This we forget.

Sometimes misery comes to you not because you

have done anything bad in the past, but because something good is going to come to you in the future.

This you must remember: tomorrow your condition may change.

Don't judge anything by success. It is the inner change that counts.

In defeat do not give up. Meditate. Think of God as best you can. Steady, steady, don't lose heart—be steady like a rock. The light of victory will be in your eyes.

"I may have failed but if I try again I can bring out the strength I need to succeed. I have it in me"—this is self-confidence.

Out of discouragement comes another kind of courage, different from the flimsy, superficial courage that exists one moment and is gone the next.

It is not necessarily the worthy person who advances in spiritual life; it is the determined person.

A person who is fully determined to pursue the spiritual life and has that as his only goal is as good as there already; nothing can deter him.

❋

Everything we do is really seeking God. Everything has a germ of goodness in it.

You need very little to go ahead if you really *want* to go ahead.

Be reminded that in every spiritual effort you are not alone: the Lord adds His weight to your efforts. You will find this to be literally true.

We never work alone. All the forces of good back our good efforts and all the forces of evil back our evil deeds.

❋

God *must* accept those who have come under His protection. He *will* listen to you. All you need is a grain of sincerity.

There is a subtle law in the spiritual world: if you

seek something, you will have it. But you must walk toward God before He will come to you.

When you struggle spiritually, even though you see no result, you are awakening the higher mind.

Remember this: whatever spiritual experience you have is forever yours, even though it may sometimes be submerged.

4

Change Yourself

In spiritual life the way is to change ourselves, to change our own reaction to things. It is our reaction that makes all the trouble.

Unless there is some change within ourselves, we cannot hope to change the objects of our perception.

What you perceive depends upon the condition of your own mind.

If you see things wrong you are swallowing poison.

It is in your own mind, the way you look at things, that causes all your misery. A little change in the mind and you will become a different person.

Change yourself. Try to live up to your best—to the truth, as you have known it.

Don't try to change the outside. Make the change within yourself.

If you want to conquer anger in someone else, don't you yourself be angry.

You cannot change anyone. There has to be a desire for change before it will take place. If the seed is not planted, you can't make the plant grow.

One who is calm can conquer ruthlessness in others.

Affirm the presence of God. Say "Lord, You are here." Change your thought.

Say always, even in anger, "I am addressing the Divine. This is the Divine." Shake hands with the Divine One. Hear His voice. Feel His presence.

When you become truly convinced of the one blissful, divine reality, the next step is to make yourself see the Divine at *all* times. Break the old habit of mind that stops short of truth. See the Real.

If you are a recipient of God's grace you must also contain His strength. Don't think that you can remain what you are—you will change. A person who says he has received God's grace but remains the same has not really received it.

5
Don't Criticize

Don't criticize others. If you judge another person, you are being judged—the same tendency in your own mind has already judged you.

You see everything according to the quality in your eyes.

If you see a fault in others, just wait a little and you will see the same fault in yourself.

Because you do not know yourself and others, all sorts of problems arise and you become confused.

A person has to have something within himself before he can see it in others.

When a person accuses others, he needs great compassion and kindness, for deep down he accuses himself. When his own faults become too much for him to face, he faults others.

Those who are apt to see faults in others do not have the power to see good in others.

A wholesome mind is incapable of seeing faults in another.

Things are almost wholly inside—how we feel, how we react—and this is what will determine our condition.

This universe is like a mirror. The way I find the world is the way I am now.

Whatever happens to me happens *because* of me.

Only cowards hate. Strong people do not have to hate in order to do their duty. A coward is someone who blames outside things.

To the extent that we learn to feel for others—to that extent we transcend our own limitations.

If you must judge a soul, you should know not just

his present surroundings and background, but all his previous background.

Let the Lord do the judging and protecting. Go forward with trust. As snow melts in the spring sun, all restrictions will melt away. You will tear the powers of ignorance to shreds.

A spiritual person should have no animosity for anyone. In seeing faults in others we are strengthening the same faults in ourselves. It is a vicious cycle and a psychological fact.

Have forgiveness and a sense of humor. Ignore things. Once you recognize hurt, you rarely forgive.

No righteous indignation—don't backbite. You will never get anyplace in religion by taking that attitude. Continually getting hurt will not lead you anywhere. Whether others behave this way or not has nothing to do with *you.*

Stop thinking about the awful things done by others and see how they change. It is a fact that if we change our own mind, other people will change.

If you think you are separate from a person, that person will make you small.

In criticizing a person you are shutting off the most wonderful truth: that person is God.

Forget that anyone is bad, that anyone is inferior. You have to go beyond the person's behavior. The real person is God, peeping through the eyes. This is the highest ideal.

Never think another person to be weak or imperfect. Behind his form lies the ever effulgent Being, the Strength of all strength, the Wisdom of all wisdom.

6

See God in All

According to Vedanta every person, every being, is perfect. We should treat every person, every being, as God Himself.

The only legitimate approach to another person is to look upon that person as God, because that is the truth.

Look upon others as divine—as God, as the Self. All sense of separation, fear, attachment, love, hatred, and jealousy will vanish forever from your heart. Of whom would you be jealous? Of God; of your true Self? The Self is all there is.

"Be still, O mind, and know that I am the Self."

Imagine God in the heart of all beings.

Every single being that exists is an inexhaustible mine of beauty and love.

Unless we see divinity in every being, we will never see unity in the world. Intelligence is that which sees unity among apparently separate things.

You can have a true democratic spirit if you can really persuade yourself that everyone is divine.

Our perception, our understanding, is only skin deep.

When we address a person, we address the skin. Address the real person—talk to the conscious, luminous, perfect Being. You will get a wonderful response. Truth has extraordinary power.

Check yourself. Never judge an appearance. Always acknowledge the luminous Being within.

Do you care for others? If not, you have a prickly pear disposition. Why can't your heart leap in joy when you see a devotee?

Cultivate the capacity to appreciate the good in

others. See something beyond. Make your heart bloom and also the hearts of others.

Be kind. Don't worry about whether this is right or wrong—be kind.

Be kind to all living beings. Serve them. You will develop a taste for the name of God. Get rid of your limitations and all beings will begin to reveal themselves as divine.

Spiritual people learn to reverence everyone.

Behind what appears to you as a dull face, a bright face, or a vicious face is God alone. All these various pictures we see are but misreadings of the one truth, just tricks of the mind. Actually, everything is perfect.

Everything brings the message of God; from everywhere comes the touch of my Beloved.

This one is dear to me not because of what I see, but because deep down in him is the resplendent Self, expressing Itself in that voice, those postures, those gestures. Consider the truth about a person and the superficial things will appear sacred—expressions of the divine Self within.

The Self dwells in the monk, in the devotee, in the foolish; so I, the Self, am enjoying and suffering in each one.

Concentrate on that which is resplendent in everyone and you will reach Oneness.

7
Be Affirmative

Always think of yourself in the best terms and try to live up to them. You will be surprised.

Always affirm the positive thing. Doubt itself is the product of ignorance.

By thinking about negative things, you strengthen them. How can you forget what you think about every day?

Don't dwell on the defects of your own nature, but rather dwell on that which will take you to Truth, to God.

You don't have to keep checking and rechecking mistakes—that is not a spiritual way of life. Just plunge into the thought of God.

Every experience contains within itself the germ of freedom. Mistakes contribute to our freedom.

Don't let regret melt in tears or evaporate in sighs. If you do, there will be no change in you. You will go on making the same mistake all your life.

If a room is dark it does not become light because you say, "Oh, it is so dark." Do not tell yourself that you are a sinner.

Whatever wrongs you may have done, however terrible you might be, still say that you are the Spirit. Affirm this until your backbone has become strong and you have become ten feet tall.

Even when you are sunk in the deepest despondency, affirm your true nature.

Remove all obstructions from your mind. The most effective way is to affirm, "I am the Spirit in thought, feeling, and action."

Feel that you are of the same nature as God—the lion's cub is leonine. True love comes between equals.

Affirm whatever attunes your mind to an awareness of God. That kind of awareness gives elation, longing, yearning. You are in love with God and cannot live without Him.

Affirm, affirm—do everything unto the divine Self! Only when the little "I" is crushed will the great "I" come out.

Affirm the true "I": Repeat, "I am not mind, intelligence, ego. I am the Absolute One—pure Consciousness, pure Bliss!"

The man of Self-realization is a master of destiny. He is positive, affirmative. He is in communion with the Infinite, rejoicing in the Infinite, serving in the Infinite. That communion is continuously going on in the heart of a knower of God.

8
Be Purposeful

Purposefulness belongs to the Spirit. Everything in your day should be purposeful.

Every morning you should think about how you are going to make that day spiritually profitable. It should be a daily resolution.

Make the most of *every* moment. The time is very auspicious. Who knows when you will have a better opportunity?

If you give up work you will rot away, but before you rot away completely you will make your environment a pure hell for everyone else.

Everything you do leaves a mark on your mind.

If you can do one simple thing perfectly, you can also do spiritual work perfectly.

There is nothing like being simple and going about it in a simple, steady way.

Do everything with full attention. Nothing should be done without reverence, for everything is really done unto God.

You should not worship God carelessly. It is not that God will punish you but that you will destroy your own fine sense of values. Don't trample on greatness in any form.

One should have reverence for whatever one does, even if it is just an extraneous thing.

9
Be Joyful

It is not in misery but in joy that one progresses in spiritual life.

Learn to enjoy God. Even if your progress is slow, enjoy it. Do not undertake your spiritual practice as a heavy labor. Think that you are fortunate because your mind has turned toward God. Look upward and adore, but also look downward and bless yourself. It is not given to everyone to remember God.

Without joy we cannot carry on for long, even though doubt may cloud it. Doubt punctuates our progress from beginning to end.

Don't let misery enter. It is sheer madness to associate spiritual practice with misery—a disease. Take this attitude: "I am satisfied. I shall do my best." Do your best and be happy about it.

Know that God is always your companion.

The glory of God knows no end. You can never come to the end of enjoying God. The experience is ever new.

When peace deepens, it becomes joy. Joy is not something separate.

When joy is intensified, it becomes love. Just as the warmth of spring fills everything with renewed life, so pure joy will make you feel as if a new spring has renewed your entire being.

Joy, power, and truth go together. The sign of power is pure joy.

Only an infinitesimal fraction of the joy of God makes this world joyful.

There is a state in which you become aware that you are free, that you are no longer a bound person.

The result that will come to you after a lifetime of spiritual practice is so astonishing that you will not think the effort was very great.

We are going through life for just one purpose: to make all the wonderful things—love, truth, compassion, joy—blossom.

The Self of man is *Ananda,* bliss. If you but catch a glimpse of *Ananda* you will be suffused with joy. Never count your powers small.

Blissful and free—such is the nature of the Self. This spiritual Self is your birthright.

10
Be Loving

The love in one's own heart sweetens everything.

If you are fully conscious of something, you actually possess it.

Learn to feel that the person you love lives beyond the façade of the face.

Learn to think in this way: "This person is the perfect Spirit."

To reflect the object of our love in our own consciousness with a sense of *adoration*—that is what love is.

All great love in the end becomes reverent. It is like the calm ocean reflecting the full moon and rising to it in the tides.

Love that is not accompanied by reverence is poison.

Every true lover grows a garden within. When a person loves God, a wonderful garden blooms in the heart.

There is a flower that blooms in heaven, and you sometimes get a whiff of its fragrance on earth.

You will find His presence like a perfume around your being.

The presence of God is everywhere, within and without, like the fragrance of perfume.

On the relative plane God can be seen, heard, touched, even smelled—like the subtle, sweet fragrance of sandalwood.

Once you taste the love of God, you will never again want to sink yourself in the love of human beings.

When you learn to love Him, all attachments are easily broken and all barriers fall away.

Cry for God! Let the heart melt and wash away the scars of a lifetime. Everything else is trash.

Crying of the heart is what distinguishes a truly spiritual person from someone who is merely moral or religious.

All that is lovable, adorable, and satisfying is contained within, in the Divine, and in infinite degree. Impress this upon your mind.

Make yourself the embodiment of peace, love, friendship, and joyfulness. Vow this to yourself. Let your face shine with the glory of the divine Being.

You cannot love God unless you think that you are the same as God—you would be afraid of Him.

Love in its fullest manifestation transcends its limitations.

Everything becomes grace the moment you shed limitations.

II

Be Strong

Shed all those things that are vulnerable. Recognize that they are nothing. The only thing that counts is that you are the Spirit.

Be strong, be manly, be ashamed of any smallness within you. It does not become you.

All miseries can be overcome—but you have to be strong. There is no other alternative.

What is strength? It is a feeling that makes one self-confident, independent, fearless, invulnerable, and capable of meeting any situation.

The goody-goody will be kicked around like a foot-ball—and not just by men. The gods, the angels, and the demons will also kick him.

When you become strong, all kinds of nice things happen to you. When you are weak, all things tumble around you. It is your own strength and your own weakness that are responsible for all the things that happen to you.

⁂

Everything worthwhile must begin with the assumption that you are strong enough for it.

Everything that finds expression has power behind it. Things are accomplished by the strength that is put into them.

All great things are the fruits of strength. Weakness never does anything for you. You have infinite strength within yourself.

There is no substitute for strength.

⁂

Strength is love. Only the strong can love; the weak can only be sentimental.

Where your heart is, there your strength is. When your heart is not whole, the power goes out of you.

Where your heart is, there you go. The heart is the fleet steed on which you ride.

Power has to be joined to love. When love is not infused with tremendous power, love becomes impotent. That is the tragedy today. People want to love, but they are so weak that they are utterly helpless in regard to themselves and to others.

You must remember: in the long run it is your stout heart that will take you to God.

Only stouthearted people will go for spiritual values. Cowards will always crawl in the dust.

Success is not always granted to the strong, but don't be daunted by defeat—that would be the real defeat.

Chickenhearted people cannot have true devotion. Only a strong person can say, "Here is Thy servant; command."

The weak *shall not* realize the truth!

With strength, approach God who is the source of all strength.

Be strong and self-reliant. God will bring the soul to Himself.

The strength of the soul has to be uncovered. We let our energies pour out.

Nothing prevents you at any time from realizing the highest, which you really are.

12
Be Brave

Courage is the essence of faith. Only the brave can have faith.

A person who wants to be religious has to be very courageous. God makes things easy in the beginning, but afterward He demands the full price.

We live in a world in which fear predominates, and next to fear, prejudice.

"Face the brute!" said Swami Vivekananda. It is more beneficial to practice detachment in the face of sense objects than to practice meditation for hours and hours.

Never fail to face facts. Never do it timidly. Remember, you have within you what it takes to face the whole universe.

The very fact that you have the courage to struggle will itself bring you liberation.

Where have you found bravery without the necessity for struggle? How can you express courage without struggle? Can you claim to be heroes if you have never entered the battlefield?

What do you know about the power of the mind until you have battled with it?

If you have struggle within you, know that God has blessed you. If you stay where you are you glide pleasantly—peace there is, but it is the peace of degeneration.

The cult of happiness is deadly for the soul. Soldiers are not sent to the battlefield with the words, "My boys, I expect you to be happy!"

When surrounded by enemies your mere goodness will not help you. You have to roar like a lion!

When people in the outside world want to browbeat

you, open your eyes like a lion and browbeat them back.

Fight like the strong, not like the weak. Fight for conquest, not for retaliation. Fight to carry something through—no more than that—and afterward, harbor no resentment.

How shall we carry the sword? We should not have any kind of antagonistic feeling toward anybody. The sense of hatred has a weakening influence that will corrode us inside.

You need a sword in your hand for the battlefields that are within and without. You have to fight every inch of the way if you want to reach the goal.

Use the sword not for selfish purposes but for the inward struggle. Bring out the sword of knowledge to destroy all wrong mental states.

Destroy your internal enemies with the sword of knowledge. The essence of knowledge is that everything is Brahman.

Carry the sharp sword of wisdom in your hand. Boldness and determination are called for. Look the universe in the eye and say, "Lord, there You are."

Keep your sword shining, your eyes open and keen. Detect what is wrong and destroy it. You will experience an expansion of being at that very moment, an elation of the spirit and the presence of the Divine.

A wise person is willing to fight his battles within himself. He eventually becomes established in a higher state of mind.

Caution is the word. Does it imply fear? Then use the word *alertness.* Alertness is the sign of the brave man.

Eternal vigilance is the price of freedom for the soul.

Inside warfare is good until you have found peace.

All real struggle is a calm thing.

13

Be Truthful

Of course you have to be absolutely truthful! How else would you know the truth?

Truth is the simplest of all.

Think of truth, know it, speak it—*become* it! Build up the habit. Be earnest.

I, the seeker of truth, can be my own lamp—gracious, dignified, courageous, afraid of nothing, hurt by nothing—bringing peace and freedom to all.

The yearning for truth is another name for love.

Unless a man lives up to his highest conception of truth, he goes to pieces.

Turn your face toward truth and hold your eyes

unfalteringly on the vision, regardless of quarts of tears. Everything false will fall away from you.

Act on truth and suffer the consequences.

Either something is true or it is false. If it is true, whether you like it or not, you have to swallow it.

Do not test truth by the joy it brings—truth brings pain along the way. Joy will come later, a steady joy. The highest attainment of truth is *pure* joy.

Truth cannot bow to anything. It is a shining sword and those who wield it must be strong. You have to be a hero.

Truth is an interior thing and you need to go within.

All coverings and darkness must be penetrated, permitting truth alone to triumph. Once truth is found, all else that you believed can be discarded.

Truthfulness leads you deeper and deeper—there is no end to it.

Truth will shatter all your illusions. It is a powerful corrosive. When you succeed in removing your identity from these illusions, you annihilate name and form. The hidden Spirit shines out.

⁂

The whole search for truth is for unity and for continuity. It is in unity that joy is found.

Let all truths come into you and integrate themselves.

Living truth is handed down. Truth flows from an enlightened person in whom true knowledge has been conserved.

Give the truth to all. It is strengthening—the most powerful medicine. Force it down the throat!

⁂

Vedanta carries us forward to unadulterated truth: everything that exists is divine.

If we want to be true we must learn to see everything as it really is—as divine.

Face the truth: the whole of existence is one universal Spirit and you are that Spirit.

Let your consciousness dwell on the supreme, eternal Being; at any moment the truth may flash out. Try and you will succeed. At this very moment you are perfect divinity!

14
Be Unselfish—Selfless

Be unselfish. Your mind will become as wide as the sky.

Unselfishness is power.

When you use every ounce of power that you have, more power comes to you.

Don't ever seek things for yourself. It is humiliating, degrading. Seek things for others.

Acknowledge even the least merit in others and magnify it, but don't *ever* expect any approval or recognition for any accomplishment of your own—be it physical, mental, or spiritual. Who cares what happens to this body-mind complex? It won't last anyway. Give it up now in your mind. Be free! The Self alone is true.

Be glad to be ignored as a person—be free in the real

Self—ever independent, alone in truth. Forget your relative existence. Lose interest in all that is transient, unreal.

I am fully convinced that until one has learned to serve a noble cause unselfishly, one is not fit for the deeper life of contemplation and meditation.

It is all very good to sit and meditate and feel devotional, but often it does not go far. You have to dig deeper and break the bondage of selfishness.

It isn't enough to be unselfish. Become the un-self—selfless!

We have to forget ourselves utterly and love Him with our whole heart.

Self-surrender—absolute selflessness—is the offering of everything to God. It is a wonderful state if it comes to you naturally. All stress, all strain goes. Your whole being cools down, relaxes. You are nestled in the comfort of God. You are in the arms of the Divine Mother.

15
Be Willing to Sacrifice

You have to sacrifice part of yourself to bring anything into creation.

Everything comes into existence through self-sacrifice. God, also, in order to bring this universe into existence, sacrificed Himself—the great meaning of the crucifixion.

We don't have the sense of sacrifice. We don't understand the great thing we are seeking, so we don't know the great sacrifice that has to be made.

It is only those who have come very close to God that He forces to make sacrifices. Toward them alone He becomes insistent. Toward others He is very agreeable. He says yes, do whatever you want to do. He knows that otherwise they will push Him away.

16
Be Free of Desires

It is desire that makes us impure, not what we do.

It is desire that has spoiled the whole world.

We must kill worldly desires before they have matured and seeded. If we do, in our next life we will be born clean, our mind will be free. Otherwise the cycle will go on and on. How do you know you will have spiritual tendencies in your next life?

Satisfying desires never satisfies desire—it only adds fuel to the flame.

Starve any action or habit that you want to get rid of.

Desires can be controlled. They may appear to sweep you away, but if you take refuge in the Lord you will withstand the current.

It is always possible to transmute desires.

Desires originate from your own being trying to fulfill itself—groping for its own truth. If you want to be free from the drive of desires, turn inside and realize them within.

Desire for experience will not stop until the conviction comes that everything is within.

If you become attracted by physical beauty, remember that within you there is much more beauty. Your infatuation will go away. That is the only way to conquer desires.

"Within me there is infinitely more love than I am seeking outside"—if a person can meditate in that way, the sense of sex will go. This is not a trick of sublimation. It is going back to the truth.

You cannot really practice the presence of God fully, with your full mind, unless you have given up desires.

You cannot take refuge in God unless your only desire is to be liberated from the bondage of the body and mind. Your whole being must want to seek God.

Practice the presence of God without desire; seek no fruits for the little ego.

Always remember that *everything* to which the mind goes is Brahman. Even desire is Brahman in another guise, disguised, a trap for the mind. When you become thoroughly convinced of this, the mind will settle down like a good boy and be content to dwell on Brahman alone.

17

Be Detached

How to practice detachment? When your whole life has been organized with a sense of duty and purpose, that clarity of thought will come to you.

Serve all with detachment, seeking nothing in return. Then everything you do will become like a meditation, will go toward God.

All worldly attachments gradually become broken— the soul just rises into the bosom of God and becomes one with Him.

In the real practice of detachment, one feels greater love, kindliness, compassion, and unity—never a lack of interest or indifference.

Antagonism to worldly life means that there is still attachment. He who conquers desire has neither attachment nor antipathy.

Our own life and the persons with whom we associate make claims on us. For a long time we put these claims alongside the unvoiced claim of God, but God's claim is the only one we should heed.

As a person advances spiritually, he first gets rid of personal memories.

Whatever you want to give to God you may not share in the slightest degree with your relatives or with the world.

Nothing could be more wrong for a devotee than to give his heart to anyone but God.

There is no one—no power or being on earth—that can make any difference to you.

It is one thing to enjoy the beauty of this world and quite another to covet it. To enjoy a flower is different from wanting it in your buttonhole.

If you can look at something and not covet it, you have become spiritual.

Not until we truly grasp that this world of relativity is darkness do we seek the light. As long as we think of the dream as reality, we remain in the dream.

Attachment to things that are not God makes the mind impure.

Attachment to God—that is what is called detachment.

18
Be of Service

This is the age in which every man has to be his brother's keeper. Serve man as God.

Conceive of all your service as worship, whenever and whomever you serve, and it will be a worthy offering to God.

All souls belong to God. We can serve, but not manipulate, them.

Don't let a single opportunity to serve God escape you.

People who fail in their worldly responsibilities are too weak to be exposed to the heavier responsibility of God's service.

Some people think they will become largehearted through participating in the broad aspects of human service. They want to do things on a national scale, but they only succeed in cramming too many activities into their lives.

It may be easier to feel that service for a religious organization is service to God, but the spirit of service is truly established only when it is extended to work done in every other walk of life.

Doing good to others is often a mask for assuming leadership. From this a subtle sense of egotism begins to grow. If you think it is your duty to help others, first get rid of your ego.

Perform your duties without the interference and upheavals of your little ego—without any trace of self-interest in your actions.

Regard all as the children of God. Learn forgiveness. Have contentment. Do not be ambitious—the ego must go. Only when you fulfill the letter of the law in all these practices can you render true service.

There is nothing like getting lost in others to get rid of the ego—serve, serve, serve, and think of the perfect Being.

Serve others as embodiments of God and you will serve them in the right spirit. Then worry and anxiety will not work like a poison on your being.

※

The knower of God alone has the power to help others. The ignorant are themselves helpless.

Without knowing the truth you cannot do any good. First enrich your inner life by meditating on God directly. Then change the pattern of your inner life by trying to see God in all beings. Transform your actions by offering everything to Him. Eliminate your ego, which is never satisfied.

Just to say that God is in everything is not enough. You must perceive God in your own consciousness.

When you awake to the presence of the Spirit in yourself and in others, then every word you say, every action you take, and every thought you think will be a source of great good. Your desire to help others will be satisfied.

※

To serve what the spiritual teacher stands for is to serve God.

Don't be a nuisance in your effort to serve the teacher. If you really want to do something for me, see me as I truly am. This is the highest service.

Service to the devotees is essential to progress.

On the ordinary plane, service to others may be motivated by love and sympathy. But when we see that suffering humanity is really God in different forms, this consciousness of the Divine in everyone is what motivates us to serve them. Service performed in that spirit is a potent means of God-realization.

Does your service to others make the awareness of God clearer within you?

Those who see the presence of God in everything may be engaged in what appear to be worldly activities. Yet in reality they have undergone a profound change through which they have become spiritual.

Service purifies the heart, but it is only the means to a greater end: the eternal realization of oneness with God.

When your consciousness is no longer bound down by ignorance and you have become clearly aware of the effulgent God interpenetrating the whole universe, you are filled with awe and wonder, reverence and ecstasy. The psychological consequence of that feeling is a profound love for all beings and a desire to serve them.

He who serves God should be full of awe.

Kneel down before Him whom you would serve. Be patient.

19

Be Silent

You must catch hold of silence. That is the clue.

Silence is the shrine of the Lord—that is where you will find Him.

Struggle in absolute stillness and silence, whether for five months or five years. Everyone has to pass through that stage. Calmly, quietly, go ahead.

The spoken word that your superficial mind receives rarely does you any good.

If you are untouched by gossip, you will be surprised at how much nonsense has gone out of your life.

Most people talk nonsense.

Our trouble is that we talk too much. If we didn't talk, we wouldn't have any trouble. All speech pre-supposes otherness. Be still. Be with Him alone.

If you don't have to speak, *don t* speak.

First control speech, then the mind with all its desires, then the ego.

We find Him in the silence when the mind has quieted down; in that silence He shines.

20
Be Calm

Be calm and accept with grace whatever comes. If you can make the mind perfectly calm, you will hear His voice deep within your heart.

The more you try to conquer the body and senses, the more they revolt. Be calm when they revolt— eventually they will be conquered.

It is easier to fight than to remain calm and in control of the situation.

Accomplishment outside is greatly inferior to accomplishment within.

All greatness comes from a calm, joyful mind. Only a joyous, cheerful heart can feel the dark sufferings of mankind.

Our satisfaction lies in making our mind attain to the infinite, the calm, and the true.

Remember this: there is no better tonic for the nerves than pure thoughts.

Calmness is necessary for the sake of knowledge.

Gentleness, calmness, peace—that is the real strength.

What is gentleness unless there is tremendous strength behind it? Nothing.

In *sattva,* poised in wisdom, one is close to the Divine. But going beyond *sattva* one is identified with the transcendental, in which alone perfect fulfillment is attained.

If you approach the state of *sattva,* imitate the ways of *sattva.* A man of *sattva* is infinitely enduring and patient. It is very natural for him to forgive and forget; it is not a sign of weakness.

The sign of strength is restraint.

Patience itself is the remedy for many things. Be cheerful and patient. Patience is the basis of cheerfulness.

When true vision develops in the soul, the senses stop. Deep within there is calmness—silence—God.

THE EXPERIENCE OF GOD

I Am the Self—Pure Consciousnees—All Light

I
Reach Higher

Don't think small thoughts. Reach toward the sun, if you have the courage.

Beware of all small things. They belong to the body and the mind. If you persist in small things you will strangle the great things to death.

By denying the small things, you achieve the great things. The great things are never taken from us. Ignore the small things. Outdo them.

When you have too much to enjoy, the outside becomes too big. Unless you make yourself bigger than the outside, you will not know what to do.

The small-minded say, "This one is my own; that one is alien to me." The generous say, "The whole world is kin to me."

It is the smallness of things that has ruined everything. If you connect everything with God it will become pure.

Renounce whatever is small, whatever is petty, whatever is limited. Renunciation should be something upon which you build up your existence.

Renunciation is the giving up of the small for the sake of the large. One cannot have both.

Every day our effort should lie in what we can do away with. Basic renunciation should be practiced always.

As long as you possess anything, you cannot be sure that you have renounced it. You do not know where attachment is hidden. An outward gesture is not necessarily renunciation.

Do not hang on to things! A new outlook will come in your life. Make a bundle of the past and drop it.

Neither give up nor acquire, but transcend—rise above everything.

If you grow spiritually, renunciation will come upon you. You will be so rich in your spirit that worldly riches will be of no value to you.

Renunciation is perception. Full renunciation gives immediate perception.

Out of renunciation comes the peace of mind that is another name for strength.

If a person approaches God with a spirit of renunciation, it is only a question of time before identification with God will come.

Wherever the light of God has broken through, there true renunciation has come. That is the one sure way to know whether a person has realized God or not.

2
Go Deeper

You are deep and profound. If you become superficial you are like dust scattered by the wind.

You cannot expect anything from people who live on the surface of life. If you do not know how to live deep, you are nothing. You are just a weight on the surface of the earth.

You have to learn it: on the surface there is nothing that is worthwhile. Nothing! Deep down, beyond the body and the mind—that is where you live.

By all means be rude rather than trivial.

The great art is to go deep, both in your own life and in the lives of others.

Make a habit of understanding everything in its essential character. Look to the real person beyond the body, beyond even the mind that finds expression in the face. Say to yourself, "I am seeing Spirit, God Himself."

If I look upon you as Spirit, not only as the body and mind, there comes another quality in my speech, in my words, in my manner.

Learn to go through the barriers of the body and senses into the realm of deep, pure emotion and inner knowledge. Then you will become simple. You will be a source of joy.

The deeper one goes, the more cheerful one becomes.

Everything that you see here is a poor and fragmentary reflection of God. Just below the surface is the profound consciousness of God. Contemplate this.

When you have penetrated the surface, everything seems to be of importance and wonderfully beautiful. This is the vision of the Soul.

We are born to realize the deeper Self. Get over the illusion that you have to live on the superficial plane.

Make it natural to live constantly on a higher plane of existence.

Everything has to be reinterpreted—our lives, our feelings for others. We must cease thinking in terms of our own satisfaction and learn to think in terms of the good and the true.

A great soul knows no boundaries, no limitations. He makes no distinctions. His sense of consistency is necessarily different from ours. In order to find *his* consistency, we must go very deep.

When a godlike man goes away, you will find your consolation only in the depths of meditation. The surface of the mind cannot reach that which the great ones embody.

The deep calls to the deep—only when you have become deep can you reach that depth.

The Ancient One is seated in a cave in the deepest part of your being. You will discover Him there.

Profound depths are within us. There is no difference between God and our divine Self.

Anyone who would have the fruits of eternity must learn to move slowly—not lazily, but deeply.

Go deeper. Make your mind come face-to-face with the Soul of the soul. Don't let it stop short. Go to the thing that will enlighten your heart.

3

Open Your Heart: God Is Always There

The temple is your own heart! Try to worship Him there. Let your eyes go within and see only Him who dwells there as the light divine. Meditate upon Him. If you do, you will not remain what you are now. You are bound to become a deeper person.

It is in the interior space of the heart that the light of God is perceived.

Seek Him within your own heart. Imagine Him there. That is realistic imagination. What is at first imagination soon becomes perception.

Even the world of the imagination is beggared by what you would actually see if your mind became free.

The heart is closer to us than reason. How can dead thought and dead intellect grasp the living God?

We are so busy with our thoughts that we do not hear the celestial music in our hearts. Every moment we are realizing God in our own immortal soul, but we do not listen.

Thou art playing in my heart. Thou hast made me the instrument of Thy music.

The heart—it is there that all the fun is. It is from there that you rise.

Unless your heart has opened up, the full presence of God in nature cannot be seen. Get rid of the idea of separation between God and nature. Then you will truly live.

The heart has to be opened by itself. It is in the heart that He is reflected. Remove the dust from your eyes. See Him.

You have got God as a prisoner in your own heart because He is the Infinite One. He has to be every-where. Whether you are good or bad doesn't matter—you have *got* Him.

He is seated in my heart and I am in His heart, too. He is not far off. I am surrounded by Him.

The only door is in your own heart. Plunge in and pass through into the heart of the universal. That is the way.

The only way to enter the Real is to enter into the heart of your own being.

4
God Is Not Hidden: Beckon Him

You know, my friend, God is not hidden. With just a little beckoning of your finger He comes out. Why not, since He is the reality of everything?

We have somehow cultivated a state of inattention. Every single one of us is having the experience of God always.

Questions such as "Where is God? Who is He? What is He?" are foolish. In that very moment, whatever you see is God. He is *here.* Rub your eyes. Clear your brain.

Unfocus your worldly vision. Rub your eyes. See that God is all there is. Spirituality is learning to focus so that you see only God.

There is not a thing that you look at that does not shine with the glory of God.

Never search for things that will remain outside of you. Things cannot become a part of your inmost being. They are not worth having.

If you want the knowledge of the Spirit, it will come to you. Take it. It is always there.

Such is the nature of knowledge that it comes without being guided by anything.

When your whole soul is filled with the reality of God, there is nothing left in your consciousness with which to perceive the world of matter.

He is within you. He is outside you. He surrounds you. You are within His arms. Can you get away from God?

Perfectly pure, one-pointed devotion to God completely disarms Him and He reveals Himself at once. God is a sucker for devotion.

He is the pure, all-pervasive consciousness gleaming through the living, shrouded in the nonliving, and shining bright in the serene life of the knower of Truth.

See the one Being that saturates the universe.

5

Quiet Your Restless Mind

A man can have everything, but if he doesn't have the cooperation of his mind, he has nothing.

Brave the danger of the mind. It has more power over you than a million atomic bombs. To control it makes you the master—fearless.

Until you have actually felt the mind at work within itself, you will not be able to control it.

Only when the mind is under your control and has become peaceful can you know what the mind is. You can never know your own mind unless you practice self-discipline.

How to bring the mind under control? Direct it so that it cannot do anything on its own, that is how.

You have to be calm and quiet and examine everything that arises in your mind. See that it is in accord with reason and not just accepted automatically by custom.

You become calm by eliminating the causes of mental disturbance. Find out what they are and get rid of them. It is as simple as that. All spiritual teachings are about how to remove disturbing things from your mind and your life.

Tranquility comes when the rubbish of the mind has been removed. Greed and self-indulgence must be vanquished.

If the mind is gloomy, why are *you* gloomy?

You have to be bold and persistent. Cut down the old thoughts again and again as they come to you again and again, and then the roots will die.

You have to examine all your motives. You will find that it takes a long time before your only motive is the realization of God.

At every step make a choice for the good. The mind

will become quiet and you will feel in harmony with the greater life, even though you stand alone.

Depth in meditation will not come without quieting the mind. The mind is quieted best by unselfishness—there is no technique so good!

When the mind is restless, you know very little of reality. When the mind is quiet, you know all of reality.

When the mind is disturbed, in that mind God cannot be reflected.

The nature of the mind is to reflect the Self. The mind is coextensive with God, transparent and luminous when it reflects God alone. Do not cheat the mind by stuffing it with other thoughts. Stop dragging the mind down to worldly things and it will naturally rise on its own to reveal the Self.

Wherever there is serenity, there is the reflection of divinity.

Calmness and purity are different words for the same thing.

Out of the infinite calmness of the mind, the knowledge of God comes.

When the mind becomes serene it perceives the unity of the universe. In the midst of the mind's furious activity, we see a thread of peace.

When the mind is perfectly still, the soul becomes Spirit.

6
Concentrate

Concentration is nothing but attention. It requires a quiet mind, not a scattered mind.

Concentrate, concentrate, concentrate: that is called willpower. Ordinarily, we let our energies pour out.

The mind becomes unified when concentration takes place.

All efforts in religion or spiritual life are designed to bring about a concentration and unification of the mind.

In serious spiritual life one of the important things is to know where the mind has gone and to gather its scattered pieces. We are not aware of the hidden pieces of the mind.

Only when we have brought some peace into the superficial part of the mind will we become aware of its hidden pieces. That is important. Layers and layers of the mind will become exposed and we will see just how scattered it is.

No one can perceive God unless he has gone through the different layers of the mind. Those who have seen God have a tremendous influence on others— they know the mind through and through.

The scattered mind is the worst state, related to the worst phase of reality.

The more unified and concentrated the mind, the greater is its power to reveal the truth and the greater is the truth that it reveals.

The more concentrated the mind, the more subtle and refined it becomes. All perception depends upon the condition of the mind.

Ordinary perception will not reveal God to us. Only when the mind has become concentrated does a new kind of perception come. When concentrated, the mind reveals not only the divine reality but the truth about ourselves; it removes false ideas.

Everything is revealed to the mind that is one-pointed.

Gather the scattered parts of the mind together and devote the whole mind to the perception and contemplation of the divine reality. The effort, if you make it, will enable you to become a lion of a man.

7

Meditate

To the extent the mind is divided, meditation will be superficial. The essential condition of meditation is one-pointedness.

Concentration is the very heart of meditation, but not all concentration is necessarily meditation. In meditation the rays of the mind must be focused on God.

When one-pointedness reaches its culmination, the crystal mind reflects pure divinity.

Meditation is different from concentration. In meditation there is relaxation and the mind is comparatively free from worldly desires.

Meditation is a slow, slow process like the opening of a flower—silent and graceful.

Meditation should be undertaken with a sense of

eternity, not in the atmosphere of time. Just feel that you and the eternal God alone are there. With that feeling you are bound to succeed.

Don't suffer from impatience. In meditation you must feel you have time or the mind will always remain superficial.

Meditation cannot be brought about by any kind of conscious forcing.

Don't let meditation become a mechanical practice. Everything mechanical is killed. To murder your spiritual practice is as terrible as ordinary murder. When you feel the very beginning of mechanization appear, kneel down. Be prayerful.

The practice of meditation must be regular, without any break, day after day, until consciousness begins to expand. The mind cannot be trusted. We do not know from day to day what we will think. We need the steadying influence of the meditative period.

If you don't meditate every day, how do you think

your soul will remain strong? Spiritual energy dissi-
pates.

If you are tired and cannot think, meditate. You will
find that your mind has become refreshed.

Our mind is part of the larger mind. When other
people begin to think, our mind becomes unquiet.
The early morning is the best time for meditation,
when other people are not yet up.

When you begin the practice of meditation, there
may be a period of stress. But there comes a period
of stability. Then, when you meditate for even a
short time you reach a deeper part of your being.
You feel as if someone has poured energy into your
body and your mind and they are filled with peace
and joy.

You go to a pool of peace and joy and strength—
that is how one should meditate.

You begin the practice of meditation with the assumption that He who is present everywhere must be here now, not far away. With this consciousness you try to feel His presence.

The body should be quiet; the senses shut in. Withdraw the mind from everything the senses bring in from outside, and from thoughts and feelings arising in the mind itself. When this is done, make the whole mind face the Spirit, which is neither within nor without but just *is.*

As you meditate on the divine form, at first it moves very much. It looks diffused. After long effort, you make it stand still. Great steadiness, calmness, stillness settles, and the form begins to glow with life. Then, it is said, He even speaks.

We must know that the form of God exists within our own consciousness. We are not imagining this, though it may seem so at first.

At first meditation is an act of imagination. This is very fruitful. Our whole life is an act of imagination.

True, in the early stages of meditation we have to use imagination, but it is not an imagination without basis in reality. It proceeds from the actuality of the divine existence.

Meditation is not imagination; it is anticipation of the Real. If He were not present, however much we concentrated we could never realize Him.

Meditation is a deliberate effort to anticipate the awareness of the divine reality that will come to everyone in course of time. That awareness is not an artificial state that we create through imagination.

Meditation is not simply thinking about God. It is an actual perception of the presence of God. Meditation is a process of perception—perceiving Him who is already *here.*

We are so blind spiritually that we do not see the divinity. But as our spiritual vision opens, we find that what seemed to be only a mental image is in fact a living reality.

Meditation is the way to perceive a higher reality.

When meditation becomes real you at once perceive a higher reality, and you have not the slightest doubt that it is a superior reality.

Meditation has to begin with reality, grow in reality, and end in reality. We must convince ourselves that He is dwelling within us. Since God is omnipresent, He must be here, too.

Because we are still obsessed by the sense of space, it is necessary to localize God in one place for meditation. It is generally accepted that the light of God is to be found in the interior space of the heart. Consistency of effort will one day bring us to that spiritual space where we will find the divine light shining.

We should meditate with the greatest earnestness. Consider even the point of courtesy. Give all your attention to Him.

If you are earnest and persistent, you will succeed. I will not say that you will realize the highest in this life, but it is enough for anyone to make steady progress.

Meditation is aspiration, the desire to see God more and more clearly. You meditate because you love Him and want to dwell upon Him. We need not try to calculate our degree of development or fitness to perceive the Divine. Indeed, it is an obstruction to do so.

You may find for a long time that your meditation is merely a groping in the dark. You don't know whether you are achieving anything at all. But just as a blind person enters a dark room and touches things until he finds what he wants, so one day in meditation you will suddenly find that your mind has touched something, perceived something, that you have never known before. Once you experience it, believe me, meditation will never appear to you as a useless effort.

You will find that one day after your meditation you will feel full of power.

We look upon meditation as the one instrument by which we can penetrate the barriers between ourselves and God and see Him face-to-face.

Meditation should not only take the form of a specific practice but should continue throughout the day. Beyond every form and function is the inexpressible divine Spirit. Push your thought beyond the form with every act of perception. Relate the thought of God to everything you do and say.

Contemplate His presence everywhere. Brood over it. Feel that sweetness, like a mother yearning over her child. Feel it! Don't seek. See! He is here.

A meditative person practices constantly the blissful presence of the Lord and, when possible, absolute identity.

How to meditate? Penetrate the depths in yourself and in all beings. Go deep and see the divine effulgence, feel the divine joy. He is the one Being. Realize this and all your fetters will fall off. Work at it! Struggle itself is a sign of growth.

Make the mind continually reach the deep level where the Spirit exists. Make a practice of driving the mind to the recognition of this adorable, exalted Being everywhere, who alone is the Real.

If you go very deep in meditation, the mind comes away from all the senses. God is not far from a mind that is free from the demands of the senses.

When one has surrendered oneself entirely to the Lord of love, the Lord cannot resist His beloved devotee; and, having for a long, long time attracted the devotee to Himself, He is at last irresistibly drawn to His devotee's love. They come closer and closer until they blend together. The Lord has surrendered Himself and embraces His own, even as the sea welcomes the stream that flows into it and becomes one with it.

The Lord is the divine wish-fulfilling tree. He gives a devotee whatever the devotee asks of Him.

Feel like a pot submerged in the ocean. You are submerged in the divine Being. You are praying that He will reveal Himself to you; that He will help you with your difficulties; that He will keep you firm in devotion, unwavering in effort. Then continue to feel submerged, surrounded, filled, overflowing.

God does not like begging. He gives Himself in response to love. The mind becomes very calm—joy is felt, then sweetness, then love. A person who is progressing in meditation feels this refreshing calmness and is bathed in an unutterable sweetness and love that will stay with him all his life.

Try to please the Lord alone. He being pleased, all are pleased. He *is* the all in all, our very Self.

❋

The highest meditation is to love God—beyond that is identity.

Those who meditate try to step into the unknown. We want something that will never bore us; for this we must be absorbed in the Infinite.

Meditate on your God, but meditate also on your own Self. That is what you really are.

In meditation you must be aware that the goal you think you are reaching is already there. You are It.

At least 95 percent of the mind must be absorbed in God—the Self, the one pure consciousness whose center is *here* but whose circumference is nowhere.

When one is completely identified with the Self, which is like pure gold, only then can one give up meditation. Meditation is necessary until then to keep the image shining, like polishing away the dirt of ignorance.

God does not care a fig whether you meditate on Him or not.

8
Repeat the Name of God

Turn your consciousness away from things. Dwell on God. Sing, repeat His name, worship Him, offer acts of service.

Repeat the name of God every moment you have free. Fill every space of your day with the name of God. Repetition is absolutely necessary before a truth can be deeply impressed upon the mind.

The name of God is somehow tied up with God Himself—if you pull at one, the other comes to you.

Learn to repeat the name of God such that the moment you say it, the whole mind is stirred up with it and the feeling of it. The mind must leap up and become colored with the name, the knowledge, and the perception of God.

Dunk the mind in God at all times in whatever way you can.

You have taken the name of God—at once you are pure.

In *japa,* repetition of the mantra, you should not be conscious of the body, mind, or any mental state. There must be full concentration on your *Ishta,* Chosen Ideal—no other thoughts—complete absorption.

Japa colors the surface of your mind. Worldly thoughts arising there become suffocated. It is like sowing oats to kill weeds.

Spiritual practice consists in removing obstacles. If you repeat the name of God, the divine reality will flash.

When *Om* is pronounced rightly, the entire universe comes with it and is swallowed up.

9
Find the Indwelling Self (The Real You)

In the heart of every being, every person, is a vast cosmic Being.

You have within yourself all the things that will make you a liberated spirit. Go and find them.

Within you, in the center of your being, is a flame— a light without any smoke. That is Brahman. Meditate on Him.

It is absolutely obligatory to achieve God-vision. So instinctive should this be with you that you judge everything in terms of whether or not it will help toward this ideal.

Remember your true nature: you are pure, perfect, free, and full of wisdom. This knowledge of your true Self is like a fire that will burn all your desires to ashes.

You have denied your own true nature. Set fire to the rope that is binding you. Make the transformation!

You realize the nature of God only when you realize that your own true nature is divine.

Power will come from within yourself. You don't have to go begging for power, for grace.

When a man realizes his true nature is divine, he clearly sees that he has been answering his own prayers all along.

Let me tell you this: if God ever gives you anything, He will also make you realize that it is coming from within yourself. It is never added unto you, for what is added can also be taken away.

If you are real, you are real because of the presence of God in you.

I am the Real, like the sky—spontaneous and steady.

If you think of everyone as a bit of sky, that is good. Think of yourself as sky, too.

We are continually trying to regain the lost memory of our true Self—that is what is called life.

Man is truly divine, pure Spirit. It is his ignominy that he forgets it, and this forgetfulness is the source of all his troubles.

Practice that you are the Spirit. There will be a carriage of your head, a look in your eyes, a smile on your lips that are not of this earth.

Say this: "When I close my eyes, there is the divine Self within my heart; when I open my eyes, there is the divine Self in every being."

You must learn to feel the divinity and the strength of divinity within yourself—there is no other hope.

10
Think of Brahman as Form,
and of Form as Brahman

You don't really meditate on the form but on the Being who is in the form. When you perceive this, you become free.

He is an infinite, shining form. Although He has a form, still He is infinite.

In infinite ways let your mind grasp God. Let your consciousness expand.

Those whose intellectual conviction is monistic but who have not reached the state of freedom from the body, what are they to do? There is a middle state: they can think first of Brahman with form. Later, they can identify with Him—that is when the true practice of Advaita Vedanta begins.

Until you perceive the formless reality, you have to take recourse to symbols.

It is Brahman Himself who makes a form for Himself, not the devotee. When you make something yourself you are greater than what you have created, and you would never find satisfaction in a God that is your own creation.

If God takes a form—have you any objection?

As long as we are attached to our own person, we shall want a God who is personal. When we have learned that we are really formless, beyond the body and mind, our heart will also seek the formless God—the indescribable Impersonal God.

If you worship the Personal God, do it like a strong person. By and by, try to transcend this personal phase and go toward the impersonal. Remind yourself that the Personal God is also the Impersonal. You will find that slowly you have gone from the Personal God to the pure Principle. It is in this way that you become established in Vedanta.

Always, if you feel deep love for God, you will also feel your identity with Him. Deep love always leads to monistic realization.

When you reach a certain state, the name of God has gone and the cluster of ideas around that name has gone. You perceive only the shining Spirit. Your mind has become pure.

Recognition of this vast Being in everyone—the ability to feel the divine presence in everyone—is the test of growth.

God created millions of forms, and into these He infused Himself.

The Infinite can be realized in the finite.

The Infinite should be known and loved in infinite ways.

We have imposed infinite forms on God. We have also imposed the reality of God on these infinite forms, and that is the reason they seem real and alive.

There are not millions of beings; there is just one Being.

Everything in existence is based on Brahman, yet Brahman is not connected with anything.

The universe is like the shadow of Brahman. Just as when we look at the shadow cast by a wall we are truly looking at the wall, so we really perceive Brahman when we look at the universe.

Bring yourself to the consciousness that what you have now is insignificant. Take possession of your birthright, which is a million times better. Realize that Brahman is all that is to be known; all that is, is Brahman.

If you think rightly, you will have glimpses of Brahman.

11

Perceive the Highest Spiritual State

There is a sort of alchemy in a high spiritual state by which this very world will become transformed from material to celestial.

One day you will find when you open your eyes that everything is an embellishment of God. You will have full awareness that wherever there is consciousness, there is God.

To catch a glimpse of the spiritual Being is to realize that no judgment, no thought is necessary. That effulgence is self-evident.

The illumined state—the natural state—is full consciousness, without a speck of darkness, ignorance, or sleep.

I would not call anyone an ideal man until he has touched the feet of God. Then all qualities become pure and innocent.

When you perceive God, there is no within and without. You cannot speak of God as being above or below. There is no direction.

When God is both within and without, even God is gone. What is left is beyond words.

Thou art *Sat-Chit-Ananda*—transcendental Being, Consciousness, and Bliss. Become identified with this.

It is only after the highest realization that you are fit for the intimate experience of God. Spiritual life begins after *samadhi,* the highest transcendental state.

Those who realize *samadhi* and merge into the Infinite water the roots of humanity.

They dwell in infinitude who perceive the formless Being.

He who, even once, with eyes wide open, has seen this whole world of our waking experience vanish completely and has known the one homogeneous light as his own Self can never again really forget his true nature, the Atman, nor ever lose his awareness of the one all-pervasive consciousness.

Coming down from the transcendental, one sees that whatever happens is just all right—all right, wonderful, wonderful, wonderful!

Really, everything is perfect.

12
Be a Light

The finite and the Infinite will never shake hands, but the body can become surcharged with the light of spiritual consciousness. It becomes the vehicle for Spirit and waits to obey Spirit.

Men are verily lamps of God. In some the light is smothered by the impurity of the mind; in others it shines bright through the mind's purity.

Impurity is that which obscures your enlightened Self.

We seem limited only because we have denied the luminous presence of God within the heart.

The true Self is the light effulgent.

As you become established, a light shows within you.

Don't let the light go out. We should be very careful.

If you light a lamp for your own purpose, it will throw light for others also.

In the darkness, the divine light leads us on more surely than light at noonday. Spirit can never be darkened.

The great ones do not do anything but this: they recognize the divinity in you and that divinity responds and comes out. Light responds to light.

SUGGESTED READINGS

The editors have selected a few books to supplement the text for readers who would like to know more about spiritual teachings in the Ramakrishna-Vivekananda tradition of Vedanta. The list includes several classics from the traditional literature, now printed in later editions. Works by Swami Ashokananda are available online in the United States at www.sfvedanta.org and in India from Advaita Ashrama at www.advaitaonline.com. (Please see www.kalpatree.com for additional books and sources.)

Ashokananda, Swami. *Ascent to Spiritual Illumination: Ten Lectures on Spiritual Practice.* Calcutta: Advaita Ashrama, 2001.

—————. *Meditation, Ecstasy, and Illumination: An Overview of Vedanta.* Calcutta: Advaita Ashrama, 1990.

—————. *The Soul's Journey to Its Destiny.* Calcutta: Advaita Ashrama, 1993.

————. *When the Many Become One: Three Lectures.* 2nd ed. San Francisco: Vedanta Society of Northern California, 1987.

Bhagavad Gita. Translated with notes, comments, and introduction by Swami Nikhilananda. 1st ed. New York: Ramakrishna-Vivekananda Center, 1944.

Brown, Shelley. *Centred in Truth: The Story of Swami Nitya-swarup-ananda.* 2 vols. New York: Kalpa Tree Press, 2001.

Burke, Marie Louise (Sister Gargi). *A Disciple s Journal: In the Company of Swami Ashokananda.* New York: Kalpa Tree Press, 2003.

————. *A Heart Poured Out: A Story of Swami Ashoka-nanda.* New York: Kalpa Tree Press, 2003.

————. *Swami Trigunatita: His Life and Work.* San Francisco: Vedanta Society of Northern California, 1997.

————. *Swami Vivekananda in the West: New Discoveries.* 6 vols. Calcutta: Advaita Ashrama, 1983–87.

M (Mahendranath Gupta). *The Gospel of Sri Rama-krishna.* Translated with an introduction by Swami Nikhilananda. 1st ed. Foreword by Aldous Huxley. New York: Ramakrishna-Vivekananda Center, 1942.

Nikhilananda, Swami. *Holy Mother.* 1st ed. New York: Ramakrishna-Vivekananda Center, 1962.

Vivekananda, Swami. *Vivekananda: The Yogas and Other Works.* Chosen and with a biography by Swami Nikhilananda. 1st ed. New York: Ramakrishna-Vivekananda Center, 1953.